Handmade
Tea Bag Folded
Greetings Cards

*In loving memory of 'Ammie' and 'Cyril Squirrel', whose legacy has been the knowledge that with good friends and family I **can** survive all things.*

To my Mum for the gift of creativity.

To Jenni, Becki, Jason, Megan and Reece, my wonderful children and grandchildren, without whose support I could not have made it this far.

To Julie, who always believed that I had a book in me, and to Maggie, who first set me on my creative journey.

And most importantly to Anna – my chauffeur, chaperone and helpmate.

Thank you all.

Handmade
Tea Bag Folded
Greetings Cards

Kim Reygate

SEARCH PRESS

First published in Great Britain 2003

Search Press Limited
Wellwood, North Farm Road,
Tunbridge Wells, Kent TN2 3DR

Reprinted 2003, 2004 (twice)

Text copyright © Kim Reygate 2003

Photographs by Roddy Paine Photographic Studios

Photographs and design copyright © Search Press Ltd. 2003

ISBN 1 903975 76 X

The Publishers and author can accept no responsibility for any consequences arising from the information, advice or instructions given in this publication.

Suppliers

If you have difficulty in obtaining any of the materials and equipment mentioned in this book, then please visit the Search Press website for details of suppliers:
www.searchpress.com

Alternatively, you can write to the Publishers at the address above for a current list of stockists, including firms who operate a mail-order service.

> **Publishers' note**
> All the step-by-step photographs in this book feature the author, Kim Reygate, demonstrating how to make tea bag folded greetings cards. No models have been used.

I would like to extend my heartfelt thanks to everyone who has helped turn my dream into a reality.

Special thanks to Wendy at Stamps and Memories for the endless supply of tea bag papers and stamps, and for the kind permission of Impression Obsession Stamp Company and Design Originals Publishing Company for allowing me to use them in this book.

To Helene from Magenta for the use of some of her inspirational stamps and papers.

To Julia at Simply Stamps and Judith at Woodware for providing me with just some of the materials with which I played.

To Tina and Karen at Cranberry Card, Sue at Craftwork Card, and Angela at Phrazzle Card for all the card and paper goodies.

To Davina at Stampcraft for providing the last minute supplies that I needed for photography.

I also want to thank the team at Search Press and John in particular for all his help in making me realize that I could do this; to Roddy for his endless patience in getting each shot just right; and to Julie Hickey for putting my name forward in the first place.

But in particular I would like to thank Anna for always being there when I needed her support or a kick in the pants to get me going when it came to writing all the words; without her help this would never have been finished.

Front cover

This is a variation of the 'Eastern Promise' card shown on pages 30–33.

Page 1

Radiant Sunflower

This bright and sunny card uses a combination of rubber stamps and mulberry paper with printed tea bag papers (see also page 23).

Page 3

Sea Treasures

Hand-stamped images were created using a dye-based ink pad and a seashell cube (see also page 40).

Page 5

Red Roses

Punched paper and vellum were combined with craft stickers for this unusual landscape format (see also page 47).

Printed in Malaysia by Times Offset (M) Sdn Bhd

Contents

Introduction

I first became involved with papercrafts at a needlecraft show in 1996. Rubber stamping looked fun and, after attending a series of classes over the next few months, I became a self-confessed 'stampaholic'. My addiction, however, did not stop with stamping and I went on to try many other papercrafts, including tea bag folding.

So what is tea bag folding, I hear you ask. It has little to do with soggy wet tea bags, it is simple origami using small decorative squares of paper. The origins of this papercraft lie in The Netherlands where tea bags were enclosed in pretty paper envelopes which were then used as the basis for creating beautiful rosettes – hence 'tea bag' folding. Tea bag papers, papers printed with small square designs, are now available specifically for this papercraft.

I started teaching tea bag folding in 1998 and I soon became known as the 'Bag Lady' because I always arrived at my classes laden with lots of bags. I have since played with, and taught, just about everything to do with stamping and papercraft but my regular students still think of me as the Bag Lady from those first tea bag folding classes.

I hope that the projects I have created show you that inspiration can come from anywhere. Just about any type of paper can be used to create a square, which can then be folded and transformed into wonderful rosettes. In fact I ran out of space for all the ideas that were racing around in my head when compiling this book.

I do not throw anything away because there will always come a time when I might need that little scrap of 'waste'. As I strive to use up all those little left-over pieces, I am constantly reminded of something said by one of my mentors – 'It's never a mistake, it's always an opportunity'.

I hope that these words inspire you in the same way.

Kim x

Materials

If, like me, you are a papercraft fanatic, you will already own many of the materials and tools needed to make the projects in this book. If you are just starting out, however, I suggest that you buy just the equipment you need for a particular project, then make more use of them by creating designs of your own. If you get hooked, as I am sure you will, you can then start to enlarge your work box.

Card blanks

You can buy packs of ready-made card blanks, but I prefer to work from flat sheets as this gives me the freedom to size a card to suit the design. A good quality, reasonably heavy card should always be used as the blanks for all projects. Suitable card is available in a myriad of different colours and textures. Choosing just the right colour can make all the difference between a good card and a truly stunning one.

Decorative papers and cards

You will need a selection of papers for card inserts and for making your own envelopes. Sheets of paper and lighter weight card are also required for layering background panels. Again, there is a vast range to choose from. Apart from plain coloured paper and card, glossy card, velvet and metallic paper and vellum are wonderful layering materials which can add a touch of elegance to your designs. Even a printed serviette can be transformed into a background paper, or folded for a rosette.

   Although you can use both card and paper for layering panels, remember that the more layers you include, the heavier the finished card. So, if you want multilayered panels, paper is definitely better.

Tea bag squares

There are lots of printed sheets of tea bag squares that can be used to make rosettes. Some sheets have just one design on them, others have two different but compatible designs. All printed sheets have enough squares to make at least one symmetrical rosette. While this type of rosette is quite lovely, I often make rosettes with squares cut from printed, random-pattern papers or from papers that I have decorated myself. You can even cut tea bag squares from wrapping paper.

You can cut papers with plain scissors.

Use a craft knife with a metal ruler and a cutting mat.

A paper trimmer is useful when cutting lots of tea bag paper squares.

Paper punches cut very accurate squares. They are ideal for punching squares from random-design papers.

Other equipment

Plain scissors can be used to cut paper or card, but more accuracy will be achieved if you use a **craft knife** and **metal ruler**. A self-healing **cutting mat** will protect work surfaces. If you become addicted, you may want to invest in a guillotine or **paper trimmer**. Very accurate squares can be cut with **paper punches** that are available in many sizes. Decorative and **deckle-edged scissors** can add interest to layered panels and help hide a multitude of sins with tea bag folds.

Bone folders are shaped tools that enable you to score and fold card to give a crisp professional finish. They also help create sharp edges on tea bag folds, which are essential when putting the papers together to create the finished rosette.

Decorative **paper punches** come in many shapes and sizes. These can be used to create identical repeat images from card and paper. One of my favourites is the southwest corner punch which I use to add just a hint of detail to a card. **Metallic thread**, wrapped round these punched corners, gives an elegant finish (see page 43).

I use **rubber stamps** to decorate cards with both solid and fine-line images. They are available in a wide variety of shapes and sizes; some square stamps lend themselves very nicely to tea bag folding. Remember your tea bag papers can be cut to any size so long as they are square.

Dye-based ink pads are quick drying and can be applied directly to the stamp. They can also be used with **fine and coarse sponges** to create backgrounds.

Embossing powders are fine granules used with an embossing ink pad and a **heat tool** to create a raised finish to a stamped image. In general, use clear powder with a coloured embossing pad and coloured powder with a clear one.

A **clean-up pad** or **alcohol-free baby wipes** are ideal for cleaning stamps. **Paper towel** or an old flannel makes an ideal drying surface for the stamps once they have been cleaned.

Use double-sided sticky tape (**DSST**) to layer card and paper, and to mount finished rosettes. A **spray adhesive** is better for fine papers, vellum and stripped-down serviettes. Join the tea bag folds together with an **all-purpose glue**, applied with a matchstick. A **low-tack sticky tape** is useful for lifting and placing craft sticker waste onto the finished card. **Low-tack double-sided tape** is used to position paper masks when sponging an area of a design. Any adhesive left on the card when the mask is removed can be gently rubbed away.

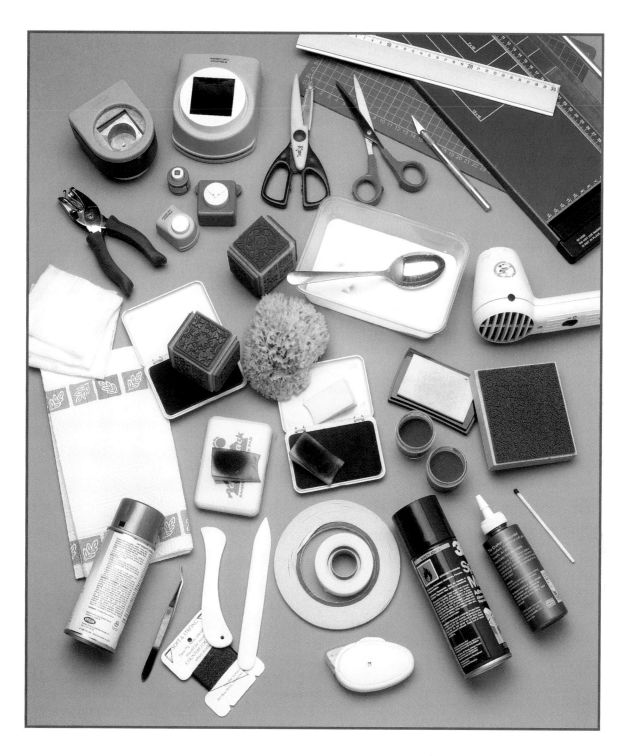

Spray webbing is a spider's-web paint finish. Shake the can well, and use a cardboard box as a spray booth to protect your work table and surrounding area.

Craft stickers provide a quick and easy way to add borders, pictures and words to your cards. Fine-pointed **tweezers** are ideal for positioning small stickers.

Always protect your work area with cheap **copier paper**. It is easy to discard when it gets dirty. I also use it to create masks when sponging and/or stamping.

Basic folds

Just three basic folds are used to make all the projects in this book: the square, the triangle and the kite. The only skills required are cutting the squares accurately (see page 10) and making crisp-edged folds. Master these folds and you can create a kaleidoscope of different designs. A single design of printed tea bag square can produce four different patterns from each type of fold. When the folds are assembled, each pattern will produce two different rosettes; one by placing the folds left over right, the other by placing them right over left. When you have mastered a fold with tea bag squares, try folding squares cut from other types of paper – a random design in each square can create a stunning finish.

Square fold

This is probably the easiest fold to start with and it will lead you on a journey of discovery. You will need eight identical tea bag squares.

1. Start by folding a paper, side to side.

2. Use a bone folder to crease the fold.

3. Open the paper, then fold and crease the other sides.

4. Open the paper, turn it over, fold corner to corner, then crease the diagonal.

5. Open the paper, then fold and crease the other diagonal.

6. Open the paper and check the folds.

7. Turn the paper over, then using the creases as a guide, start to close the fold.

8. Flatten the paper to form a small square. Repeat steps 1–7 with the other seven papers, ensuring that each square has the same design at the front.

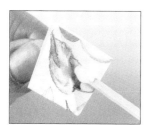

9. Apply a dab of all-purpose adhesive.

10. Insert another paper snugly inside the first so that the bottom points are aligned. Here I am assembling the folds left over right.

11. Close the fold, and press the glued pieces together.

12. Repeat steps 10–11 with the other six papers to complete the rosette.

One design of tea bag square can create four different square folds, each of which can be assembled to produce two different finished rosettes.

The open sides of the square folds in the left-hand column were trimmed with deckle-edged scissors before being assembled (see page 14).

Triangle fold

This fold is made by reversing the steps used for the square fold on pages 12–13. It is probably the most versatile of the three folds in that, with a little modification, it can be used to create non-rosette shapes (see pages 42–47). You will need eight identical tea bag squares and deckle-edged scissors to trim the open edge of each triangle fold.

1. Fold a paper corner to corner. Use the bone folder to crease the diagonal (see page 12).

2. Open the paper, then fold the other corners together and crease the diagonal.

3. Open the paper, turn it over, then fold it side to side.

4. Fold and crease the other sides, then open the paper and check the folds.

5. Close the folds to form a triangle, ensuring that your chosen image appears on the front face. Repeat steps 1–5 with the other seven papers.

6. Use deckle-edged scissors to trim the open edges of the fold. This neatens any uneven folding.

7. Referring to page 13, apply a dab of adhesive to one fold, then insert a second fold snugly inside the first. Ensure that the bottom points of the folds are aligned.

8. Close the fold, and press the glued pieces together. This example shows a left over right assembly.

9. Repeat steps 6–8 with the other six papers to complete the rosette.

One design of tea bag square can create four different triangle folds, each of which can be assembled to produce two different finished rosettes.

The open edges at the top of the folds used in the right-hand column were trimmed with deckle-edged scissors before being assembled (see page 14).

Kite (or nappy) fold

This fold is slightly more complex than the square and triangle folds, not in the folding, but in the assembly of the rosette. You will need eight identical tea bag squares. The folds must be assembled at the correct angles (see step 8) so that they form a tight circle. Any deviation will make it almost impossible to perform the final manoeuvre, and a lopsided or buckled rosette will result.

When using printed tea bag squares it is essential to decide which of the four corners is to form the points of the rosette; the first fold must be made through this corner.

1. Fold a paper corner to corner through your chosen top point.

2. Open the paper, take one of the sides across to the fold line, then carefully crease along this diagonal.

3. Repeat with the opposite side to form this shape.

4. Fold the bottom point up as shown.

5. Open the fold, turn the paper over, then fold up the bottom point along the crease made in step 4. Repeat steps 1–5 with the other seven papers, ensuring that same design appears on each fold.

6. Turn the paper over and apply a small dab of adhesive to the right-hand corner of the fold as shown.

7. Turn the paper over again and insert the glued corner in the top of the centre opening of a second kite fold . . .

8. . . . then carefully slide the paper down until it is positioned as shown. Working clockwise, repeat steps 6–8 to assemble the other six kite folds.

> In this demonstration the kite folds were assembled right into left. If you want to assemble the folds left into right, apply the adhesive to the left-hand corner in step 6.

9. To attach the last fold to the first, turn the rosette over and dab adhesive on to the exposed corner of the last fold . . .

10. . . . turn the rosette over again and carefully bring the last fold to the front . . .

11. . . . then slide the glued corner of the last fold into the opening of the first.

One design of tea bag square can create four different kite folds. Each variation of fold can be assembled left into right or right into left (see steps 6 and 7) to produce two different finished rosettes.

The two top sides of the folds used for the rosettes in the right-hand column were trimmed with deckle-edged scissors before being assembled (see page 14).

Starburst

Often, when creating a card, I do not have a finished size in mind – it just seems to evolve. I therefore tend to use flat sheets of card which I score and fold, then trim as necessary. In this project I use this method to create a square card, but it can just as easily be used to form any shape or size.

An insert adds a professional finish to a card and, if a dark colour has been chosen for the card, a lighter, compatible coloured insert will enable the greeting to be seen.

Be proud of your work and sign the back, and don't forget the poor envelope. It is so much nicer if it has been embellished to match the card.

You will need:
Sheet of printed tea bag papers
A4 (8¼ x 11¾in) sheet
of cream card
Green and yellow paper
Gold craft stickers and
tweezers
Plain and deckle-edged
scissors
Craft knife, metal ruler and
cutting mat or rotary trimmer
Bone folder
DSST, low-tack tape and
all-purpose adhesive

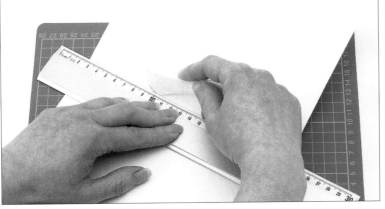

1. Mark the centre point on both long edges of card, then use a bone folder to score across the card between these points.

2. Fold and crease.

3. Cut the folded card to a 14cm (5½in) square.

18

4. Cut two 8cm (3¼in) squares of green paper. Place DSST on the back of both, then peel back the ends of the backing paper and fold to form tabs. Position one green square on a slightly larger square of yellow paper and firm down the exposed tape.

5. Hold the green square in position, pull off strips of backing paper, then firm along the edges.

6. Trim the yellow square to leave a narrow border all round. Repeat steps 4–6 with the other green square and another yellow square.

7. Use four strips of DSST to secure one of the yellow/green squares diagonally on the front of the folded card.

8. Mount the second square over the first to form an eight-point star.

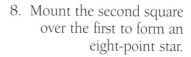

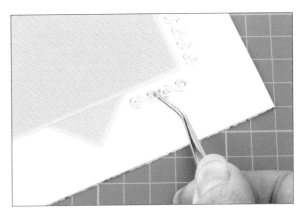

9. Use a craft knife to trim the craft stickers to the desired length, then use tweezers to lift the sticker from the backing sheet.

10. Place the sticker on to the card.

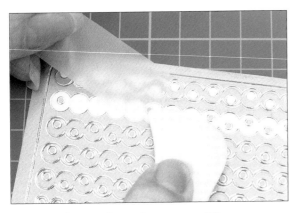

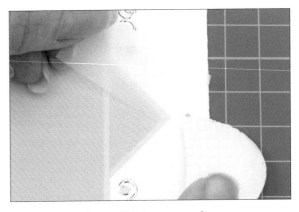

11. Use low-tack sticky tape to lift some waste dots from the backing sheet.

12. Use the bone folder to apply pressure through the low-tack tape to transfer the dots on to the card.

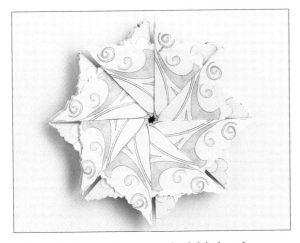

13. Referring to the triangle fold details on pages 14-15, fold eight triangles and assemble them as a rosette.

14. Use two strips of DSST to secure the rosette in the middle of the eight-point star.

15. Referring to page 18, fold and cut a piece of green paper to create an insert. This should be slightly smaller than the folded card.

16. Place DSST on either side of folded edge of the insert.

17. Remove the backing tape and secure the insert in the folded card.

The finished card together with a matching gift tag and envelope.

Tea for Two

Tea bag papers, printed with cups and saucers, were used to form the triangle-fold rosette on this card. The edges of each triangle fold and those of the blue paper that forms the base of the layered square were trimmed with deckle-edged scissors. The gold borders are straight-line craft stickers.

The card and its matching envelope were embellished with cutouts from the left-over squares of tea bag paper.

Shoe Shuffle

This three-fold card uses a tea bag paper printed with a shoe design. Quite often, when you first look at a tea bag paper design, it is difficult to visualize what the finished rosette will look like. Do not be put off by the subject of some designs that you come across – you will be amazed how different they look when folded and formed into a rosette.

I sandwiched a sheet of gold paper between the folded burgundy card and the burgundy panels on the front and inside faces of the card. I fixed the rosette to an eight-point star (half gold, half burgundy) which was then attached to the front of the card.

The matching gold envelope was decorated with small strips cut from the border of the tea bag papers.

Radiant Sunflower

I combined embossed, rubber-stamped images, bright yellow mulberry paper, and dark green velvet paper with sunflower-design tea bag papers for this single-fold card.

The envelope was handmade from a sheet of mottled gold paper and decorated with scrap pieces of the materials used to make the card. It is quite easy to make your own envelope templates, and they become specially useful when a card ends up as a non-standard size.

Shades of the Orient

Background papers can be created from just about anything. I used a brass stencil and green embossing powder on gold mottled paper to produce the floral design background for this single-fold card. Printed tea bag papers with a Chinese-character motif were used to form the triangle-fold rosette.

Blue Squares

Combining colours from the blue range of the spectrum with white trimmings gives a really fresh look to this card.

I have used one of the many wonderful printed random-pattern papers on the market combined with square punches to achieve this fresh look. Because the paper chosen has a random design, the punched tea bag squares will not be identical and so each card created will have its own unique appearance.

You will need:
A5 (4¼ x 5¾in) single-fold blue card
Printed patterned paper
Plain blue and bright white paper
White daisy craft stickers and tweezers
Large square punch and a southwest corner punch
Rotary trimmer or craft knife, metal ruler and cutting mat
Deckle-edged scissors
Bone folder
DSST and all-purpose adhesive

1. Use the square punch to cut ten squares from the patterned paper, then, referring to pages 12–13, make eight square folds. Use deckle-edged scissors to trim the open edges of each fold.

2. Cut a 6.5cm (2½in) square of bright blue paper, then use the corner punch to decorate its corners . . .

3. . . . and those on the remaining two squares of patterned paper.

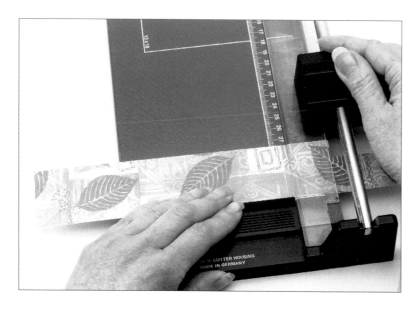

4. Cut a 4.5cm (1¾in) strip from the remaining part of the patterned paper. Here I am using my paper trimmer, but you could cut the strip on a cutting mat with a craft knife and metal ruler.

5. Use strips of DSST to stick the square of plain blue paper, and the strip and two squares of patterned paper to a sheet of white paper. Leave gaps between each piece.

6. Use the deckle-edged scissors to cut out each shape leaving a narrow white border all round.

7. Stick a strip of DSST along one edge of the white paper, and use the deckle-edged scissors to trim off a very narrow strip.

8. Use the paper trimmer (or a craft knife and metal ruler) to cut another thin strip from the remaining piece of paper (with the DSST attached).

10. Attach the thin deckle-edged strips of white paper to the card.

9. Using four strips of DSST on each piece, attach the long strip and the two squares of patterned paper to the folded, dark blue card, then attach the square of plain blue paper.

11. Referring to pages 12–13, assemble the eight square folds into a rosette.

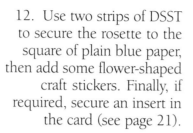

12. Use two strips of DSST to secure the rosette to the square of plain blue paper, then add some flower-shaped craft stickers. Finally, if required, secure an insert in the card (see page 21).

The finished card together with matching envelope and gift tag.

Blue Leaves

The rosette on this card was made from the same patterned paper as that for the card on page 27, but this time I used sponging and rubber stamping (see pages 36–39) to decorate the plain single-fold card with a similar design. I mounted the triangle-fold rosette on layered squares of blue paper edged with white. I turned each successive layer through 45° to echo the eight points of the tea bag rosette.

The matching envelope, the colour of which reflects the dark blue in the rosette, has a sponged and stamped band of decoration bounded by two lines drawn with a white pen.

Daisies

This variation of the basic design of the card on page 27 was made using another patterned paper. Totally different effects could be achieved by using other colour schemes.

The plain white envelope was customised with small scraps of the materials used to make the card.

28

Purple Shoes

Here again, I combined tea bag folding with my love of rubber stamping. The rosette was made from the tea bag papers used for the card on page 22, but here I used square folds rather than triangular ones. The long panel of textured magenta-coloured card was stamped and embossed with images of shoes to match those on the tea bag papers. A decorative punch was used on the corners, then the card was layered on gold and maroon paper. The square panel, on which the rosette is mounted, was embellished with corner punching and metallic thread.

One of the corner punches used to decorate the square panel on the card was also used to embellish the panels on the matching envelope. A cutout of a shoe from a tea bag paper completed the envelope design.

Blue Roses

A random-pattern paper and matching vellum were used to make this card and gift tag.

Large and small punches were used to cut the squares for the rosettes, and they were separated with an eight-point star cut from pearlescent vellum. A square of the pearlescent vellum was also used for the base of the layered panel. The top layer was decorated with a stamped design, and embossed with multicoloured embossing powder.

The decoration on the single-fold card was hand drawn with a glitter pen.

Eastern Promise

Inspiration for a card design can come from all sorts of places – as soon as I saw these serviettes I knew exactly what I wanted to create with them. Serviettes can make great backgrounds, as in this case, but once you have attached them to paper (using a spray adhesive) there should be nothing to stop you tea bag folding with them. Serviettes are usually two or three ply, and you must always separate the top, printed layer from the others before sticking it to paper. You do not want the top layer to come adrift once it has been stuck down.

You will need:

Single-fold black square card

Gold and white paper

Serviette

Rubber stamp cube

Brass detail embossing powder, embossing ink pad and heat tool

Clean-up pad and paper towel

Scissors

Rotary trimmer or craft knife, metal ruler and cutting mat

Bone folder

Spray adhesive and DSST

1. Carefully strip away the top, printed layer of the serviette.

2. Using an old cardboard box as a spray booth, apply spray adhesive to the sheet of white paper . . .

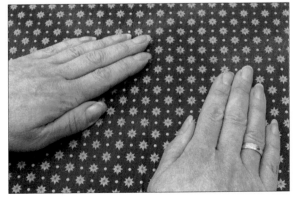

3. . . . then place the printed layer of the serviette on to the adhesive and smooth it down with your hands.

4. Cut a 6cm x 13cm (2¼ x 5in) rectangle and a 6cm (2¼in) square from the mounted serviette, then use strips of DSST to attach these to the gold paper.

5. Trim the gold paper to leave a narrow border round the square and down the long edges of the rectangle. Use strips of DSST to attach the rectangle and then the square on the single-fold black card.

6. Dab clear embossing ink on the stamp . . .

7. . . . then stamp an image on to the sheet of gold paper.

8. Sprinkle brass detail embossing powder over the stamped image . . .

9. . . . tap off the excess powder . . .

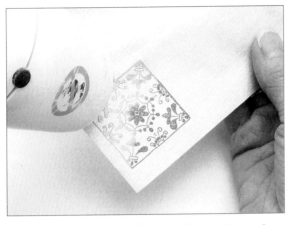

10. . . . then use the heat tool to emboss the image. Leave to cool.

11. Repeat steps 6–10 to make a further seven images, leaving a gap between each. Cut the stamped images into squares.

12. Referring to pages 12–13 make eight square folds, then, using small pieces of DSST (rather than adhesive), assemble the folded papers into a rosette.

13. Use two strips of DSST to attach the rosette to the card.

Tips for cleaning rubber stamps

Baby wipes are ideal for cleaning rubber stamps, but must be alcohol-free.

A damp stamp-cleaning mat can also be used.

If you ever apply waterproof or archival inks to rubber stamps, a solvent-based cleaner must be used.

NEVER clean your rubber stamps under the tap!

14. Fold and trim a gold insert to size, then use strips of DSST to attach it to the card.

The finished card with matching gift tag and envelope.

Oriental Flower

This card is a combination of rubber stamped and embossed images, torn strips of handmade, patterned paper and a square-fold rosette made from printed tea bag papers.

Golden Vellum

Glossy black card, matt red card and vellum decorated with red spray webbing (see page 42) were used for the panels on this square card

The rosette, also created from the decorated vellum, is a variation of the normal square-fold rosette. Here, I used scallop-edged punches to cut four large squares and four small ones. The rosette was assembled using alternate large and small squares.

Golden Orient

The rosette used on this card was made from a slightly thicker paper than normal, on which the design had been rubber-stamped and embossed. The thick paper led to a larger hole being left in the centre of the rosette, so I glued on a button to hide the hole. Having made the rosette, I searched for a suitable card on which to mount it. I came across the perfect answer in a three-fold aperture card with a gold circle that matched the size of the rosette. I did not need the three folds so I stuck the top two layers together with strips of DSST.

Eastern Delight

This is a variation of the serviette card (see page 33). I always try to customise the envelope for the finished card by using some of the left-over materials to embellish its edge.

Terracotta Tiles

Getting just the right colour of card or paper can make or break a project and so when all else fails, I make my own. A combination of butterscotch, terracotta and cranberry dye based inks have been used to create both the paper on which the tea bag images have been stamped and also the background to the finished card. This technique is a particular favourite of mine, but can be quite messy, so you might want to wear plastic gloves.

You will need:

A5 (4¼ x 5¾in) single-fold white card

Two sheets white paper, cranberry-coloured paper and black glossy card

Gold border craft stickers and tweezers

Rubber stamp cube, butterscotch, terracotta and cranberry dye-based ink pad

Fine and coarse sponges

Clear embossing powder and heat tool

Clean-up pad or baby wipes and paper towel

Rotary trimmer or craft knife, metal ruler and cutting mat

Southwest corner punch

Bone folder

DSST

1. Use a fine cosmetic sponge and butterscotch ink to apply colour randomly to the sheet of white paper.

2. Now sponge terracotta ink randomly over the butterscotch ink.

3. Change to a coarse sea sponge, then apply a random pattern of cranberry ink.

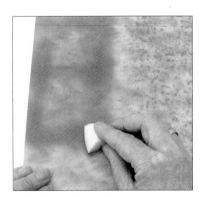

4. Use the fine cosmetic sponge and terracotta ink to create two 8cm (3in) squares of darker colour at one end of the sheet.

5. Use cranberry ink and the stamp cube to stamp eight square images at the stippled end of the decorated sheet. Leave a small gap between each square.

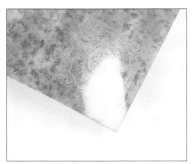

6. Use cranberry ink to stamp another image then, while the ink is still wet, quickly spoon on some clear embossing powder.

7. Gently tap the paper to shake off the excess embossing powder . . .

8. . . . then use a heat tool to set the embossed image. Leave to cool.

9. Using a craft knife, carefully cut away the corners of the embossed square. Retain the corner pieces for use as decoration in step 18.

10. Referring to pages 16-17, use the other eight squares to prepare a kite-fold rosette.

11. Tear a sheet of scrap paper in half to leave a rough edge (here, yellow paper is used for clarity).

12. Temporarily secure one half of the paper to the front of the single-fold card.

13. Sponge the exposed part of the card (see steps 1–3), then use the stamp and cranberry ink to create a random pattern.

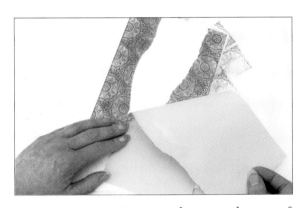
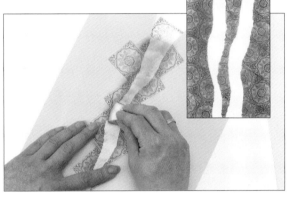

14. Repeat step 13, using the second piece of the scrap paper to create a similar random pattern on the other side of the card.

15. Now use both pieces of paper to create a pattern through the middle of the card.

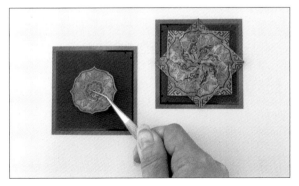

16. Corner punch two 6.5cm (2½in) squares of cranberry paper, use DSST to attach them to slightly larger squares of black card, then trim this to leave a narrow border. Attach the squares to the dark area on the sponged sheet, then trim to leave a border all round.

17. Attach the rosette to one of the squares prepared in step 16, and the trimmed embossed shape to the other.

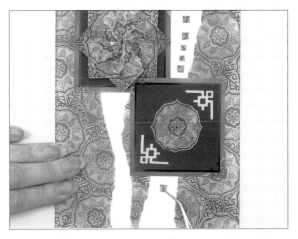

18. Attach the two squares to the card, apply decorative corner-shaped craft stickers as shown, then, using tweezers, carefully glue two of the pieces trimmed off in step 9 to each of the decorated squares.

19. Finally, cut some small squares from the sponged sheet and attach these to the white spaces on the card.

The finished card, together with matching envelope and gift tag.

Sea Treasures

An unusual rubber stamp cube with beautiful seaside images inspired me to create this card. I combined embossing with pale blues to give a wonderful seaside feel.

Spring Fever

I used printed tea bag papers to make the kite-fold rosette on this card. Before assembling the kite folds, I trimmed round the flower shapes at the top of each fold to create a completely different finish.

I mounted the rosette on a layered octagonal panel, the colours of which echo those on the tea bag papers.

40

Bugs

The wonderful stamped and embossed bugs on the square panel of this card were coloured with pearlescent paints.

This kite-fold rosette was made using squares cut from some of my own handmade background papers. I did not want the rosette to overshadow the bugs, so I used a smaller square punch than usual to make the tea bag squares.

Festive Tree

The basic triangle fold can be modified to create shapes other than rosettes. One of these is the tree shape used as the focal point of the design for this project.

When using paper punches, you can maximize the use of your paper by turning them upside down. Working this way enables you to see exactly what you are about to punch out. It is particularly useful when a repeat design is required. If you find the punch hard to use this way up, a small block of wood (the back of a rubber stamp is ideal) placed across the punch will give you better leverage.

You will need:

A5 (4¼ x 5¾in) single-fold green card

Green vellum, gold card and red velvet paper

Gold straight-line craft stickers and tweezers

Large rubber stamp with a holly design

Gold detail embossing powder, embossing ink pad and heat tool

Clean-up pad or baby wipes and paper towel

Scissors

Rotary trimmer or craft knife, metal ruler and cutting mat

Green glitter spray and gold spray webbing

Red metallic thread

Medium square and small holly shape punch

Bone folder

DSST

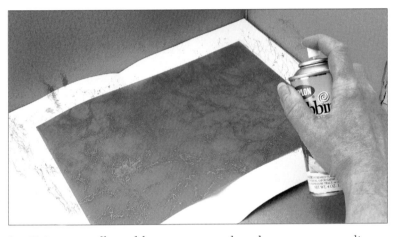

1. Using a cardboard box as a spray booth, spray green glitter and gold spray webbing on to the sheet of green vellum.

2. Punch ten squares from the sheet of spray-decorated vellum.

3. Referring to page 31, stamp and emboss the holly design on to a sheet of gold card. Trim to the edge of the design. My stamped image measures 85 x 95mm (3¼ x 3¾in).

4. Punch the corners of the embossed gold card, then use DSST to secure the end of the red metallic thread to the back of one corner.

5. Bring the thread up in the notch, take it diagonally across the corner and down through the other notch.

6. Bring the thread back up through the first notch.

7. Now take the thread across to the other side of the card and down through the notch in that corner.

8. Repeat steps 6 and 7 until the thread is back at the start. Secure it to the DSST on the back of the card.

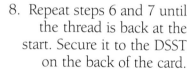

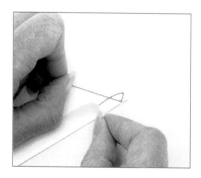

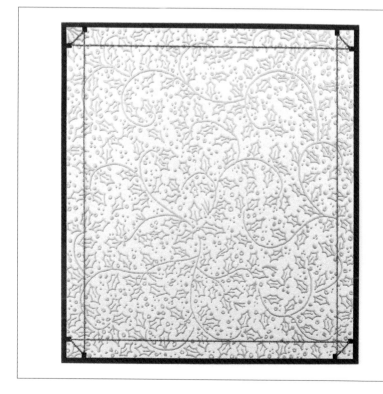

9. Mount the gold card on to the sheet of red velvet paper and trim to leave a narrow border all round.

10. Punch a strip of six holly motifs in the red velvet paper. Use the edge of the punch to help achieve equal spacing.

11. Cut the punched red velvet paper to a 25 x 14.5cm (10 x 5¾in) rectangle, attach this to a piece of plain gold card, then trim the gold card to leave a narrow border all round. Use DSST to secure this strip, then the embossed panel to the single-fold green card. Complete the background with straight-line craft stickers.

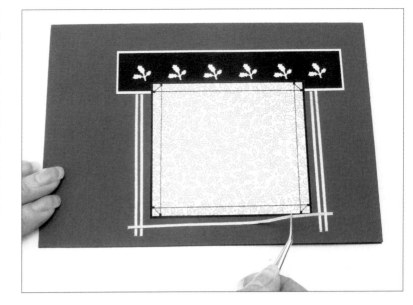

12. Referring to page 14, prepare triangle folds from the ten vellum squares.

13. Modify each fold by folding the bottom left-hand point up to the top . . .

14. . . . followed by the right-hand point. Use a bone folder to make the creases.

15. Attach a short strip of DSST on the back of each folded triangle.

16. Remove the backing strip, then start to assemble the tree by inserting one fold in another as shown.

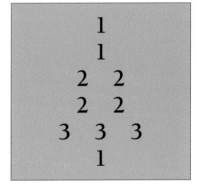

This diagram shows how the ten modified triangle folds are assembled to form the tree.

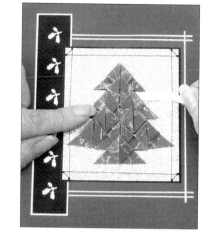

17. Referring to the diagram opposite, continue building the tree, layer by layer.

18. When the tree is complete, use strips of DSST to attach it to the gold panel on the card.

The finished card together with matching envelope and gift tag.

Far left, above

Seasonal Rose

I used a small punch to cut the squares for the green vellum rosette and a large one to cut those for the red rosette. Sprayed green vellum, decorated with one of the many wonderful punches available, was also used for the top of the layered panel. A touch of elegance was added with gold thread wrapped through the corners (see page 43).

Far left, below

Red Roses

The same combination of papers as above was used for this landscape folded card. Scallop-edged square punches were use to cut the squares for the rosettes. Gold straight-line craft stickers embellish and highlight the layered punched squares.

The envelope is handmade from a sheet of patterned paper I created myself using the sponging technique described on page 36.

Left

Forest Green

The squares used for the tree on this card were punched from a piece of green paper on which I had stamped and embossed a leaf design.

The background panel was handmade from tissue paper decorated with spray webbing and mounted on white paper.

This card would also look stunning in gold and browns with, perhaps, the addition of some small punched leaves.

Index

Terracotta Too!
This card was created in much the same way as that described on pages 36–39. Although I used the same cube to stamp the squares, the triangle folds created a smaller finished rosette. This led me to modify the overall shape and size of the completed card.

48